To all dogs everywhere and the kids who love them!

About This Book

The photographs in this book were taken with a digital SLR camera, with a fish-eye lens and flash, inside an underwater casing designed for surf photography. The photographer uses bright yellow casing to attract the attention of the dogs. He does not use scuba diving breathing equipment for photo shoots—he holds his breath underwater for up to ninety seconds at a time.

This book was edited by Connie Hsu and designed by Phil Caminiti with art direction by Patti Ann Harris. The production was supervised by Virginia Lawther, and the production editor was Christine Ma.

The text and display type were set in VAG rounded.

Little, Brown and Company ❖ Hachette Book Group ❖ 237 Park Avenue, New York, NY 10017 ❖ Visit our website at www.lb-kids.com ❖ Little, Brown and Company is a division of Hachette Book Group, Inc. ❖ The Little, Brown name and logo are trademarks of Hachette Book Group, Inc. ❖ The publisher is not responsible for websites (or their content) that are not owned by the publisher. ❖ First Edition: September 2013 ❖ Library of Congress Cataloging-in-Publication Data ❖ Casteel, Seth. ❖ Underwater dogs : kids edition / Seth Casteel.—First edition. ❖ pages cm ❖ Summary: Photographs and simple, rhyming text reveal what goes on beneath the surface as various dogs swim to fetch their favorite toys. Includes facts about the different dog breeds depicted. ❖ ISBN 978-0-316-25558-5 (hc)—ISBN 978-0-316-40103-6 (e-book) [1. Stories in rhyme. 2. Dogs—Fiction. 3. Swimming—Fiction.] I. Title. ❖ PZ8.3.C2796Und 2013 ❖ [E]—dc23 ❖ 2013015550 ❖ 10 9 8 7 6 5 4 3 2 1 ❖ PHX ❖ Printed in the United States of America

With special thanks to Nicole Simon and her wonderful rhyming talents

Seth Casteel

UNDERWATER DOGS KIDS EDITION

LB

LITTLE, BROWN AND COMPANY
New York   Boston

When I look underwater, what do I see?

So many doggies

looking at me!

Life's simple things are what dogs enjoy.

There's nothing better than fetching your toy.

Keep your eyes on the prize.
Don't drift astray.

The ball is only a paddle away.

We're just getting started.
The fun doesn't stop.

Who's ready for a big belly FLOP?

Down,

down,

down it goes

It's right below
your doggy nose

Give me your paw!
What a glorious dive.
You deserve a **doggy high five!**

Grinning,
happy,
full of joy.

You just found
your favorite toy!

It doesn't matter who gets the toy in the end.

Swimming is best when done with a friend!

Oops—missed it!
Where'd it go?

The ball was here a second ago!

Show me your smile.
You're having fun.

Everyone loves
a day in the sun!

Now try to relax and go with the flow.

Sometimes it's best to take it slow.

Catching that ring
sure was a breeze.

Look at the camera.
It's time to say
"Cheese!"

A day in the pool helps you unwind.

Here you can leave all your worries behind.

THE SWIMMERS...

JAKE, American Pit Bull Terrier

RAIKA, Belgian Tervuren

NEVADA, Border Collie

ROCCO, Boston Terrier

REX, Boxer

WRIGLEY, Boxer–Plott Hound Mix

DAGMAR, Chesapeake Bay Retriever

OSHI, Cocker Spaniel

RHODA, Dachshund

TAG, Dachshund

HERBIE, English Bulldog

CALLAWAY, Golden Retriever

American Pit Bull Terriers: These active and athletic dogs were originally bred to work on farms. One of the most famous pit bulls was a World War I hero named Sergeant Stubby.

Belgian Tervurens: These dogs are very observant! They're especially great as search-and-rescue dogs, helping rescuers find people who are lost.

Border Collies: Smarty-pants! These are perhaps the smartest breed of all. In fact, one border collie named Chaser learned the meaning of over a thousand words!

Boston Terriers: These dogs are known as "American Gentlemen" because of the kind and caring attitudes they have toward their owners. They also are known to snore!

Boxers: Oh boy, oh boy! Boxers are extremely playful! They got their name because they enjoy using their paws to bat at any challengers.

Chesapeake Bay Retrievers: *Quack, quack!* These dogs are great partners for duck hunting. They originated from two puppies that were rescued from a shipwreck in the Chesapeake Bay.

Cocker Spaniels: These dogs are known for their big, floppy, furry ears. You might recognize this breed from the Disney animated film *Lady and the Tramp*.

Dachshunds: These dogs are famous for their short legs and long bodies, which is why they're nicknamed "wiener dogs." Digging is their instinct, so watch out for holes!

English Bulldogs: They might seem grumpy, but don't let their tough exterior fool you. Bulldogs can be very friendly and easygoing. And they enjoy slobbering on everything!

...ON LAND

CASTER, Golden Retriever

CLYDE, Golden Retriever

DUKE, Jack Russell Terrier

LULU, Jack Russell Terrier

RUBY, Labradoodle

APOLLO, Labrador Retriever

BARDOT, Labrador Retriever

KING, Labrador Retriever

WARDEN, Labrador Retriever

DUNCAN, Pug

MYLO, Rottweiler

BRADY, Yorkshire Terrier

Golden Retrievers: Good boy! Golden retrievers love to hang out with people, and they love to play fetch. That instinct comes from being such good helpers to hunters.

Jack Russell Terriers: These little dogs are known to be feisty! They're high-energy, they love attention, and they're great at learning new tricks.

Labradoodles: These hybrids of the Labrador retriever and the poodle were originally bred as guide dogs for people with allergies. So if fur makes you sneeze, these are the dogs for you!

Labrador Retrievers: These dogs are the most popular breed in America and can be yellow, black, or chocolate in color. Labs' webbed paws make them strong swimmers.

Plott Hounds: What's that smell? These dogs have amazing noses! Their long ears help waft odors up off the ground, which makes Plott hounds great at finding and tracing scents.

Pugs: These little dogs have big personalities! Pugs originated in China and are known for their fondness for kids, as well as their curly tails!

Rottweilers: Sometimes these dogs look tough, but they love to clown around. They are also one of the oldest types of herding dogs, likely dating back to the Roman Empire!

Yorkshire Terriers: These dogs may be small, but they are scrappy, brave, and spunky. They love to cuddle and sit on people's laps. And they have fabulous hair!

A NOTE FROM THE AUTHOR

One day in 2010, I was photographing a dog named Buster in his yard in California. The photo shoot was supposed to be "on land," but Buster decided he would rather jump into the pool. He jumped in over and over again, chasing his favorite tennis ball. I thought, *WOW! I wonder what he looks like underwater.* So I jumped right in! I had so much fun taking pictures of Buster in the water that I decided to swim with and photograph other dogs, too. Since then, I have worked underwater with more than three hundred dogs of all shapes, sizes, colors, and ages. Most of the dogs featured in this book had never been underwater until they met me, and some had never even been swimming. Not only did they participate of their own free will, but they also had a ton of fun!

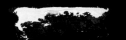